ASH

Acknowledgments

Artbeat: "The Axe" (video and broadside)

Concrete Mist Press Anthology: "Stand" and "Soldier"

Constellations: A Journal of Poetry and Fiction: "Enticed," "Crow," and "Room"

First Literary Review-East: "Hanging"

Gargoyle: "On Top of His Stomach, a Boat Was Floating" and "1994"

Ibbetson Street: "The Axe" and "Crawling Stones"

Muddy River Poetry Review: "Inhalation," "Gravity," "Deeply," and "Pedro"

Nixes Mate Review: "What If God Is Strict," "Plastic," and "Flying"

Nixes Mate Books/Broadside Series: "Burned Beyond Recognition"

Our Poetry Archive: "Air" and "Rise"

Pratik: A Magazine of Contemporary Writing: "Baked" and "Light"

spoKe: "Grave," "The Crosses," "I Don't Think of You," "Sky," and "Veteran"

The Rye Whiskey Review: "Missile" and "Escape"

Unlikely Stories: "Barely"

Writing in a Woman's Voice: "The Crosses" and "Exit"

A heartfelt thank you to my dear friends Karen Friedland, Renuka Raghavan, and Catherine Sasanov for help with editing many of these poems. You are the best! Thanks for always being there for me and for your friendship throughout the years. I would be lost without you.

Gratitude to Dzvinia Orlowsky and Flavia Cosma for your support of my poetry and friendship throughout so many years.

Special thanks to R.J. Jeffreys and Annie Pluto for your friendship and support of my writing. I appreciate our many laughs.

Thank you to Richard Feinberg for your proofing. I am so grateful!

Thank you to Doug Holder, Harris Gardner, Zvi A. Sesling, Somerville Arts Council, Somerville Artbeat, Lloyd Schwartz, Heath Brougher, Cindy Hochman, Karen Neuberg, Nina Alonso Hathaway, Richard Peabody, Beate Sigriddaughter, Michael McInnis, Yuyutsu Sharma, Kevin Gallagher, John Patrick Robbins, NilavroNill Shoovro, and Jonathan Penton for giving my poetry a home.

To my friends Carol Schmidt, Sandy Shipp, Janie Gregorich, and Shirley Prescott, thank you for always being encouraging.

I am so grateful to my Dad, Bill, Kellis, Richard, and Alexander who are supportive of me no matter what I do. You keep me going!

Thank you to Ami Kaye for publishing *Ash* and your belief in my poetry. You have made me so happy! I am on cloud nine!

Appreciation to Steve Asmussen and all the Glass Lyre staff. You all are absolutely amazing!

For Bill, Dad, Kellis, Richard and Alexander

The monster is sitting next to me, and it's so crowded in there,
the membrane between me and the events of the world is going to burst.
—Lidija Dimkovska

CONTENTS

BURNT

I.

BAKED
II.

BURIED
III.

OPPOSITION

IV.

BURNT

I.

PLASTIC

1.
X was only two months sober and was telling everyone he had a date.
Despite being told to concentrate on his sobriety and not women,
he would not listen. The next day, he said they went out for dinner.
Afterwards, she invited him to her place for coffee. When they walked
into her apartment, there were dolls sitting at the kitchen table, on the
couch, in the bedroom, and even on the toilet. Doll eyes watching him.
Creepy. He left. We all teased him and said he should have kissed a doll.
There would be no heart beating. All he would have to do is keep his lips
closed. Then there would be no feelings.

2.
X was sitting in the car with his date, about ready to go to dinner when
she said, "Wait! I have to wrap my head up in tin foil! It is important for
me to communicate with the aliens." X looked at her in disbelief. He took
the tin foil box from her and wrapped his head up with it, waiting for a
miracle.

3.
It has been a while since X went out on a date. He sat in the car with
her as she smacked her gum and then stuck the chewing gum on the
dashboard. Then she dug out her lipstick from her purse. X was still
focusing on her gum on the dashboard. He looked around her car more
closely and saw gum stuck all over the place. He felt a knot in his stomach
and was disgusted, got out of the car without saying a word. About a
block later, as he was thinking, he reached in his pocket and unwrapped a
piece of gum and chewed…

4.
The sirens were going off. X knew it was time to get out. His heart was
beating quickly. X was scared he would not make it. Heavy black smoke
was filling the apartment up. He jumped and realized it was just a dream.
Next to him was a woman, young and very pretty. His heart smoldered…
He thought, what did I do to deserve such a thing. Just then, a fireman
knocked down the door and *resuscitated* him. There was no girl. Just a
firehose through the broken window. Sometimes X, a flame is just a
flame.

Inhalation

Smoke is everywhere.
Down on the floor, I crawl.
Where is it coming from?
To be found out later...

Once outside, a fireman helps me.
Gives me an oxygen mask.
"Breathe slowly," I'm told.

As I lie there in an ambulance,
I remember your words.
They caused an explosion, this fire.

Belongings are smoldering.
It was so harsh even a firehose could not
cool down the remains.
All left uncovered, exposed to the elements
frying.

PROTECTED

Inside the house was his life,
protected by a roof.
By the time the firemen got there,
it was gone.

He sifts through what remains,
eyes sunk, hands asleep,
brain idle for hours.

The man surfaces his heart.
He carries it away delicately.
It still beats, and he breathes asking
how much sorrow can this heart take?
There is never an answer.

BITTEN

I was bitten by your heart, injured and
burnt by the flame.
The crackling was so loud, it hurt my ears.
Did I listen to my own voice which was clear?
No. I should have taken it seriously.
Everywhere I went in the house were his clothes,
his books, his life, which I let dust collect on.
Things got smokier, battling the embers with
false waters.
It did not work.

Tomorrow we find each other's breath
faithfully flowing in the wind.

Rise

Smoke rises so I crawl on the floor.
Where is the door?
He locked it—
made it disappear from sight.

He will never wake up.
How does that feel?
This place now buried by plows,
ground up, tossed like my heart.

What is left is not much
I've lost my patience for this place
Good it burnt down
My clothes are tattered, boots muddy
from the firehose water.

The next day, I return to look
To witness the aftermath
Wondering where they took his body
I am not as sad as I thought I would be.

It is windy outside.
The garbage truck is full.
Pulls away grinding.

The air feels brisk today.

BURNED BEYOND RECOGNITION

Eyes of rescue turned out to be false.
Who needs rescue?
The thought of that makes me quietly
go away from the doorway...
running from any Sonata you could play.

The house became ash from the couch burning,
the windows shattering, and glass breaking
into air.

The fireman's foam, water puts the flames
out that engulfed us.
Long sentences burned my skin.
No bandages helped.

Wrap the gauze around your tongue.
Choke, until a different sound comes from your voice...
an urgency of edges—
sharp as the mirror shards you look into.

Murderer

A catalogue of names...
I call you.
Reveal that sentences are not complete.

My skin was burned by your compulsion
to be famous.
Poor thing, the numbers look bad for you.
Somehow, you crashed into the roof and it buckled.

Life is a conviction for us.

In this apartment, which was blessed, the
angels shiver.
They know what you are like.
They open their wings and wrap me up like
a cocoon.
You are left with a burning head, and death because
it is your turn to go without a blanket, no covering,
no window open.
Everything closed.

BARELY

Pulled from the fire, unconscious,
skin blackened, filleted,
sliding off skin
You burnt me

Barely alive, thinking of how it was between us,
laughing at things that only we got
What happened that your flame became destructive?

Over and over flesh burned
You could never catch up with yourself, even
when hosed with water
You drowned

No, I will not throw you a life preserver.

RECOGNITION

You set the fire.

Everything crisp.
Ashes for 60 years, hearts
burning...

You lost your hunger for fame.
Whoops, flame.

Loneliness came from destruction.
Only one color came from your photographs,
black.

No images appeared.

Enticed

George was abstract in his thinking.
Thought everyone should understand him.
Rambling sentences about fire.
Flesh coming off bones.
It was all he could talk about.
We all know the consequences of burning.

It was the smell of burnt flesh that enticed him.
George set fires wherever he could.
Watching people escape, watching them burn.
Monster.
Cease. Stop.
The abyss will cast him into the infinite.
George killed too many hearts.

Extinction happens quickly.
Buried to the earth, George found out,
the fire hydrant doesn't work.

THE AXE

Eventually, all hearts stop.
The population is going down.
Too many fires not put out.
Too many songs not completed.
Existence turned downward…

The fireman's axe hits hard.
Slivers of wood, broken windows, no glass
showing a reflection, wants sight.
Nothing but smoldering.

It is a somber condition with water being
incapable of saving.
Hearts, shattered.

MESSES

How many messes do I have to clean up
for what comes out of your mouth?
After the fire died out, the ashes were swept.
No house, no clothes, no furniture, no books, nothing left.
No sign of us living there.

Life is funny sometimes.
It takes fire after fire until the water comes.
It was cool, soothing, beautiful and glowing.

Unfortunately now, there is only the dimness
of the sunset, happening too many times.

BALANCE

Looking over all that was burnt
I see shadows.
I wonder what has happened to the wall they were on.
Now there is a procession with ash
leading the way.
Saying goodbye is required.

No more curtains to open or close.
Our life was like that but now there
are no windows.

I'm not mournful, just relieved.
All these memories where you don't belong.
Over and over you fall crying about
all you lost.
Only words, words, words
but only one fits you.
Bastard!

PLOWING

Plowing the earth for hearts is rough.
Every day, there is death, ashes spread.
Sometimes over the ocean, sometimes on farmland.
When dead, it is good to feel a sense of home.

On the edge of the beyond, will you anxiously await me?
What can I say? I have never forgotten you.
There is so much unknown.
Will the endurance pay off?

FACTORY

The body is weak,
susceptible to illness.
A factory, where humans
stand in line as earth
runs out of room?
What will kill them?

So many buried.
No one visits the graves.
Yet their stones become tourist attractions.

Someone left a Coke on the top of
one grave.
They could have poured it into
the ground.
The soul wanted a drink but
the soil remains parched.

ASHES

Bury me into your heart.
Don't forget.
Even when you distribute my ashes.
Embers of arms will flow out into the wind.
What will I attach to.

The rain will push my ashes to the ground
mixing them with mud.
Stepped on, maybe someone will bring
me home on their shoe, wipe the mud off with
a rag, throw it away, then off to the dumps.

This is all I am, garbage!
To be buried again into non-existence.

There is a chance I will be recycled.
Later, I could be part of that doll
your child embraces.

Sky

The dark sky attacked my heart with
the only thing it knows, lightning.
Such a pounding in my chest, despite
being half-burnt, my valves still beating.

When the wind blew into my face,
I could not breathe.
My gasping, loud.

Finally, when the rain hit,
I was drowning in the drops.
Saturated.
There was little hope for me.

When the sun returned,
I was gone.
The air was crisp, the sky clear,
like when someone dies, the emptiness
is always there.

BAKED

II.

AIR

Is there no more hope for the brave
voices shouting out?
There are tears for the widowed families,
for those who lost friends, and prayers offered.
Why is there such violence?
Hate?

People strangling the heart out of existence
until only valves lay in the street.
Events are bloody.
Broken bones stay broken.
Killing is natural for some.

Fires set to burn out buildings.
The heart cold with anger.
Rage engulfing life.
Not everyone believes in destruction.
All the heart wants is to beat.

Angel, wrap your wings around the oppressed.
Hold and protect against evil and the hands entangling
the last breath…the last gasp…

The dead bodies cannot sing,
therefore, the world is empty.

Carrots

There is blood on my hands
from the knife.
It was an accident I said as I
sliced the carrots into tiny roundness.

You lost your appetite.
Blood will do this.
I took the carrots to the sink seeing
water mix with redness.

I pictured a long coffin with water inside,
soaking a body.
The sink was drained, carrots thrown out.
Orange circles in the garbage.

You banged your hands on the table.
It was legitimate.

Exit

I hide from you in ways
you'll never know.
In this empty house, it is easy.
You were condemned a year ago
because the sky went dark—
stars exiled.

All life is dying, even the pavement
we walked on.
OK, this is a lie,
but is it?

I sit on the same porch every day
wondering how many times you will
go out, come in.
A dance of the angry.
No perception of song.
A bleak fire burning on the stove,
in the fireplace, in your eyes.

Your skin will not provide an exit wound.
Stay miserable.
Aloneness is verified.
You open your mouth to talk but can't.
The void looms deep, scorched
like the desert blowing aimlessly.

BAKED

With a rolling pin in my hand,
I roll your heart out flat...
stop it from beating.
The redness of blood turns to wax,
sticky while wet.

I mix it with flour for consistency,
mind you, you never had this.
Skin is added for extra flavor.

After cutting up a few veins,
my creation is ready to bake.
Once out of the oven, all crisp,
all beautiful...
The door is opened, and I throw it out
for the birds.
Peck away my friends.
Eventually, all men get flown.

I Don't Think of You

I don't think of you,
not even in my dreams.
There is no existence between
your heart and mine.
Your heart I carved up
in the thick air.
Pieces rain down on the lawn.
Dead with no color, not keeping the yard beautiful.
Just something that blends in
over time.

THORN

You weighed me down.
Your intelligence, exhausting.
In this hemisphere, aloneness strikes,
an emptiness, a hollow heart shaking.
You are a thorn, hurtful.
Condemned, you realize you aren't the one.

TRIED

I wrote you a letter but it burned.
Tried to call but the line was dead.
Went to our favorite place but found it closed.
Thought about you but that ended.

My arms hold the air now.
It is light, non-dramatic.
It is a force I did
not have with you.

Quietness, calmness appears constant.
A withering happens as I bloomed.

STAND

Slowly, I stand
spending my time getting out of my chair
Hands and feet fight for equality
One day, the hands are stronger, next day,
the feet
Under the couch, dust bunnies are running
by my step, smashed into floorboards
sticking to my sock
Life has to fight for survival
Self-portraits for remembrance of how a life is

Smile pretty against the light, disappear
under your skin
Slowly, I stand

GRAVITY

Dampness brings a chill to my body.
Bones aching, scraping against muscle.
A violin of permanence.
Noise giving birth.

With a clenched fist, can't undo it.
I try to relax but gravity is about to
free me into space…
People will look at me day and night
and ask, "what is it?"

There is no control over what happens.
The cathedral is high and my freckles
fell on the floor as I left.
Paleness now, that no one sees, but in
the universe, I will be a prism.

Room

Walking into the living room,
the TV, couch, pictures, chairs,
are all watching me.
Watching every move, every gesture…
So powerful, my bones shudder.

I am a martyr in my own place,
weeping for all the rooms I changed.
Years of different apartments and only a few
objects remain, wondering when their time
is up, wondering when they will be discarded to disintegrate,
or will they go someplace else where spiders take refuge.

All they can do is watch a web being
weaved in the dark.
I am sorry, but this room matters.
A hunger surrounds us, dust gathers, and is
wiped off, space evading all this as
songs of the wind come through
the window and we all hum.

A Thought

I am drinking a glass of water. Maybe I shouldn't have. When the fire started, I could have saved one piece of paper with that water. The fire hydrant did not work. Now, I look at this burnt-out shell, where memories were. How can my mind possibly remember them. Mementos of you. The heart is a funny thing. I tried to cling to you but am now holding an empty glass. Maybe I should keep it filled with water. I need to keep the heart moist.

CRAWLING STONES

He was an insensitive bastard, with his
heart a stone, his eyes, a stone, his legs, a stone,
his arms, a stone
Crawling stones reaching

I got scratched, an achy body, every time
I was with him.

Once in a while, I would take one of his stones and
throw it across the river, watching it hop across
the water, sinking…

One gone, many more to go.
One by one, in the water, to the bottom
of the river bed.

He finally drowned and me, I soared
like a bird, flying across the water, singing.

DISLOYALTY

Disloyalty came early—
an inherited present.
The family deputizing the body
with abandonment.
Thoughts of love, dead.

Hands, now terminal.
Eyes, refrain
There is nothing to see.

It is no use.
Existence beyond light.
Crawling on the floor
Merry-Go-Round.

TICKET

Come get your ticket to expire.
Your lover wants you.
Take this drug, he says, it is good for you.
It only has 10 side effects—
if you're lucky, you will never forget me.
It will cripple you or kill you with yearning.
If you feel numbness or start to die,
go to the nearest ER.
Whoops, too late.
Guess you shouldn't have taken the pills.

Missile

When the torpedo hits, it is
inevitable that there is disintegration.
This is what happens to a heart when
goodbye is said.
There is a smoldering that never goes out.

You wait for it to happen again.
As you wait, the torpedo flies—
looking for someone to hit.

It is always there.
Waiting to ignite.

Buried

III.

WHAT IF GOD IS STRICT

I am looking for the right flesh with no bleeding
My voice free, hanging from the crucifix
Passion from these lips igniting sins
to clot my mouth

Crucifixes break every day,
are shoved into a drawer,
collect dust in a thrift shop
Sometimes Jesus becomes so dusty that cleaning
him is a problem
The dust too thick to let him resurrect

When he does, he sneezes?
Maybe Jesus will develop an allergy,
a miracle of life

THE CROSSES

We have broken crosses
in our drawer.
Why are they still here?

It is a sin to throw out the symbol
of Christ.
We would fall from grace.
The sacraments received on Sunday
would be for nothing.

So here they are, buried by papers,
screws, ink pens, pennies, a few rubber bands—
How sad. Christ defending himself
from junk.
Where is his heart?

Take the crosses out.
Let *him* breathe.
Put the pieces in every room
out in the open, each one
giving testimony to your life.

ESCAPE

Trying to escape, but I am surrounded by flatland.
No place to go.
If I stand behind the tree, you will find me,
behind the barn, you will find me,
behind the house, you will find me.

You would not expect me to hide
down by the Illinois River or in the
caves of Starved Rock. I will be there until
my body decays.

I will become a beautiful plant.
When you walk past, I will
give you a rash.

Hanging

We sit on the tracks with our feet hanging off the bridge.
Not worried if a train comes. After all, we will feel the vibration and run.
It is peaceful, quiet, and there is a calmness our hearts liked.
In the air, there is a scent of someone's fireplace burning wood.
Logs burning away the love they had.
Nothing lasts forever.
We sure didn't.
The smoke continues, suffocating.

LIGHT

Surrender to the dark night
where the blackness empties
into the light.
It is over between all the hearts
that yearn.

No streetlights will guide those searching
for a path.
Stones have disintegrated.
Dirt is mud and weak legs cannot walk.

Love is something that only convulses.
Empties the brain of reason.
Hear the sounds from throat.

Scream to the black sky, the endless sky, the abyss—
All else is prohibited.
Give up. Close your eyes, and beg for a light kiss.
Keep your mouth closed.

Bouquets

I have rebellion in my heart.
Veins are cold, tears passionate.
Please cover my eyelids because my
body is screaming. Cells are plowing
into cells against brittle bone.
Bringing me bouquets of lumps.
I want to talk but am empty of fire.
Silence is my calm.
Is your tenderness toward me unfinished,
undeclared or empty?

I left the window open and at
the moment of death…
I can't sleep
stand
laugh
or do anything.

The marigolds are blooming this
time of year. I bought violets instead and white
roses to celebrate one more day.
Living a life that was supposed to
be taken away, I feel crazy with power
Surviving was expected. Friends wandered ahead
of me in their grief.
Are they disappointed I'm still here? Am I at my funeral alive?

Sometimes life isn't fair.
I understand this.
Death decided to wait around and is
warm from dancing…
I am dancing with you until it is impossible
for us to separate.

FLYING

Flying on a plane,
I could touch Heaven…
clouds at my fingertips,
kissing the weightless passion.

When they shot you in the head,
cut off your arms, no praying
could be done.
All the things you wished,
there was no time for.

Death calls, surrender falls
into a void of nothing,
an abyss of air.

The plane crashes…
Sunlight stretches rays
into the earth's eyes.
Sorrow visits…burns.

TIME

I see different endings each day,
like an improv play.
Time passing…
At night, the color of lights vibrate,
forms come and go.
Light, dark, busy, empty,
performances by people—
immortality.
I can forgive the city.
Forgive the power it has over me.
I am outstretched, on fire, drowning…
Finally, I take my place beyond the edge, the world,
placed beyond the visible.
A city, standing still while I watch time and…
emerge unburied.

DOOMED BY THE NUMBERS

It was all a matter of time.
The decision was made.
For me, it was over.

How many days left in this saga?
Until the days spill into one another?
Blackout.

It is like the final curtain call
except I didn't get a final bow,
a standing ovation, cheers saying, bravo!

Instead, just another human being, disintegrating
into nothingness, who everyone thought too morbid.
That is good.

The fact is people will still go on brutally
killing each other.
Who will take my place and write about it?

By now, you should have realized, we are numbers.
The pills you have been given won't keep you alive.
They have destroyed me and as my organs fail,
I can see the CEO of the insurance company
going on a boat cruise laughing.

LIQUID

54 days until the new year arrives. I can hardly believe it. The snow packs the earth and hides the ground so well engulfing it in white. A blanket, that hurts the eyes but is still beautiful to look at. When it starts to melt, becomes just water, a liquid, it is gorgeous in another way. It changes into another form arriving differently under my boot. I gaze at it, welcome the change. Soon, it will dry up, and I will miss it. Somewhere it will disappear like you did. My heart is sad to think of it. Beating with sharp pain, I never did ask for a memento as I watched the water go down the storm drain.

PEDRO

I stabbed his heart
        through his ear
like a mysterious purring cat

This is the consequence
you face Pedro for spitting
        like a camel

Disgusting!

Which way do I wander?

Blood on my hands, clothes, hair, and face...
I know very well my ruthless side
Me, a passionate girl

escaping in your dark water

1994

I tolerated this road feeling tortured.
Somehow, ending up on a current, drowning, gasping for air.
My sorrow tightens around your neck.
There is an equation between us…you=me.
Some things are beyond the dark room we entered.
It is spring, and we released each other into the blossoms.
My scars, invisible.
Day after day, the heart is strangled,
floating on water, waiting to be laid to rest.

CROW

Every summer, days last longer
making more killing easier.
The crows cry.

Black feathers angry...
their sound, havoc
as bullets scream past.

Sick of this, I long for winter snow
burying the dead in ice a little longer—
avoiding stench.

There are weeping marches by the people,
that tumble the bodies over, frozen
transforming hospitals into vineyards
to greet grief in a bottle.

The birds stroll quickly
grabbing a worm before disappearing.

Weapons show in the faces, eyes dark with murder,
turn away.
Gather yourself, bullets are flying on
this hot day forcing skin to connect...
tricking the body into ashes.

Doesn't matter what country you are in.
Run from the dead who sleep to live.

Run

The yearning to run is over.
Goodbye sweet ones.
I put up makeshift crosses
for you.

I did not sign up for this.
Fragments of body parts still
haunt me.
I lay out roses for you daily.
The military won't admit what they
did is wrong.

Brutality, murder of the innocents.
I need to somehow take all these
bodies and pieces to a new place.
Create a new image.

ALBERT

Albert was crazy
History for the global world
A hermit wearing loafers

A bottle of wine in a brown
paper bag, he yearned for it
Sometimes Vodka, Whiskey, Rum
It all got his adrenaline going

Mild-tempered, Albert rambled about
world produce
His language compartmentalized into
words, "drink, eat, death, monster…"
He laughed, quenched his thirsty throat
swigging unfairness into his gut

In his own world…
It has to feel good to own
the dark alleyways
"Sit down," he says
We face tight hands around the bottle
and drink until narrowly slipping
into someplace else

On Top of His Stomach, a Boat Was Floating

A flower out of hell nailed his coffin shut. Someone paying respect to his dead body kneeled. It was a "she." She wore the color red and inside, her embryo wore the flag. She felt like a loser being stung by a million bees. One morning, she wore white, aqua and green, but most days blue. Why red today? These colors accommodated sensibilities and took away her awkwardness. Emotions were always down to the core. Life was a pattern with motion. She felt like she was in a whispering opera. Nothing in her life ever materialized. A paper-thin brunette, down to a skull, she kneeled by the coffin, with eyes closed, everything was erased.

SOLDIER

Flashes in the mountain
Green with white, soon red
Throat burning—
Thirst, only a thought
in this circled earth

The gunner shoots with a pumping force
A new reality hugging his heart
No time for weeping
No time for worry
No time for dying
No time for...
No time...
No.

DEEPLY

Helmet, dark eyes, dirty face
Firing, fierce bullets
hitting too much skin

Landscape, buildings flat
Sky gray
Home is doomed

Bleeding war into the earth
Hands remember, mind searches
Silence hurts, ventures into loss

Past is now, footsteps red

The world sleeps
          rests
          is tired

Sorrow heavy, sadness marches
into some splendor only imagined.

VETERAN

Focus your eyes on the knife.
You need to know where it is going.
It will penetrate deeply.

It is noon.
You want to remember the time
for some reason.
Time of death or time of living.

All you can remember is seeing blood on your boots.
It will never come off.

Focus your eyes on the smoke
in the distance.
It will never disappear.
When you make it home,
it will follow.

Focus your eyes on your life.
Why is it chaotic?
Night has cast its darkness on you.
Images never forgotten.
You vomit.

Time seems to have stopped.
No going forward or going back.

Now there is a gun in your hand.
The trigger is pulled.
The last thing you see is
blood on your boots.

WITHOUT PEACE

The dead have gray skin
Ashes fall on them today
Church bells ring dreamily as the survivors weep

Life is empty, hollow
Wind ceases
The world forgets this place

Witness the remains beneath us
Today, dirt is thrown on bodies
Fragments of lives lost mix with the
blood of the innocent

GRAVE

What is stirring in my soul?
My body drifting
unfastened with damage

Pain breaks, uncovers
the powerful depths of water
carrying me soaked
with explosions

I can't speak to the susceptible,
to the inside,
silent and buried
defending my individuality

In daylight, I leave guessing
At night, I leave armored
At 2:00AM, I grant you falling stars
beacons of the forgotten

Encampment is an experience
A human condition
My hands submerged in darkness
calculate my time left

Let me spell it out for you
in vowels you don't understand—
The earth isn't sustaining me,
my organs, which push out
into space
Bones sing to the moon,
a melody so clear, cold,
it hurts of a secret

You know so little,
the death of the mountains, the crisp
humiliation of dead leaves,
the clouds of a bad storm and rain,
speaking in punctuations nuzzling me,
while I fold closed,
the foliage disintegrating
into a remembrance

You will forget me

Now abandoned, left alone in
a cemetery,
alone in the grass, in the soil, on a
vacation in a bottomless highway,
lament like a meteor leaving a
stone, broken in pieces
like me

OPPOSITION

IV.

A/K

K sliced open his stomach.
"Blood drips," he said.

His heart was biting for love.
He had a deadline to make.

Do not misinterpret this.
Immorality is rationed.

His story ended before he could do any more.

A heard he died.
Water was quickly thrown on the ground.

She needed to put out her fire.
A looked towards the field.

Saw a cow just standing there.
She would only eat salad sprinkled with basil.

J/M

J loved fake names.
He was a burnt-out novelist.
Wrote too many stories about
horrific blind dates.
He was a wild man.
Too many plastic bags in his kitchen.
He would kill you, burn you, pretending
it was love.

M, an elementary teacher,
went out with **J**.
She thought he was popular,
would bring her wealth.
M was wrong.
Her fate lay at the water's edge.
An alligator.

Y/E

Y accused ghosts of haunting him.
He was inspired by little toy soldiers.
Y fell into the farmer's field with honor.
The farmer found him all tainted with sadness.

E loved sitting in a fictional room with
fictional poetry.
She was the queen of supernatural miscarriages.
E lit a match.
The sky turned red as she
moaned about a paper revolution.
Why was **Y** invisible?

S/A

S was in exile and drunk.
He could not forget about his
exotic lover.
Turbulence, violence, attached to him.
The spell of booze executed him.

A had eight children by S
The children cawed while looking into the mirror.
A played dead when they did this.
How could S leave her?
Her mouth was singing.

O/E

O was the master of confessions.
He would tell of fires he started.
Felt a sensual tinge watching.
This tradition was romantic.

E was very complicated.
Did not want to hear what **O** said.
There was too much ash torturing her.
She romanticized her objects, was mad
he destroyed them.
The volcano developed.

R/N

R liked tea in the afternoon before
he went fishing.
Sometimes the crisp air mortified him.
He would sit and build a fire.
One by one he took the worms
and burnt them.
He was grateful for such beauty.

N thought she could allure him
to stay home in fishnet stockings.
It never worked.
She fell into this routine daily.
The police later found her dead,
not much left on top of a woodpile
with fishnet stockings on the ground.
I guess **R** was paying attention.

I/V

I lost his tongue because of essential words.
He wore a raincoat all the time
to prevent a rain plague from touching him.
This is his consequence from twisted shame.
He broadcast too many strong burdens.

V constantly scraped her knee when he spoke.
She had to do something.
Witnessing black air from his mouth,
it was time to close the corridor.
She was destined to bring forth the divine.
V slashed his tongue off and shouted fire!

ABOUT THE AUTHOR

Gloria Mindock is the author of *I Wish Francisco Franco Would Love Me* (Nixes Mate Books), *Whiteness of Bone* (Glass Lyre Press), *La Portile Raiului* (Ars Longa Press, Romania) translated into the Romanian by Flavia Cosma, *Nothing Divine Here*, (U Šoku Štampa), and *Blood Soaked Dresses* (Ibbetson). Widely published in the USA and abroad, her poetry has been translated and published into the Romanian, Croatian, Serbian, Montenegrin, Spanish, Estonian, Albanian, and French. Gloria has been published in numerous literary journals including *Gargoyle, Web Del Sol, spoKe, Constellations: A Journal of Poetry and Fiction, Ibbetson, The Rye Whiskey Review, Muddy River Poetry Review, Unlikely Stories, Pratik: A Magazine of Contemporary Writing* and *Nixes Mate Review* and anthology. Gloria has been awarded the Ibbetson Street Press Lifetime Achievement Award and was the recipient of the Allen Ginsberg Award for Community Service by the Newton Writing and Publishing Center. She received the fifth and fortieth Moon Prize from *Writing in a Woman's Voice*. Gloria was the Poet Laureate in Somerville, MA in 2017 & 2018.

Gloria Mindock is a poet with singular vision: in *Ash*, a human heart is rolled out, then baked, then thrown to the birds; broken crucifixes are shoved into junk drawers and gather dust; a spurned/murdered woman turns into a beautiful plant that gives her ex-lover a rash. With mordant, Pinter-esque wit, Mindock explores just how far love, and even human decency, can unravel—to the point of arson, to the point of war.

Ash begins with a series of poems about lethal house fires that may be literal or metaphorical ("my skin was burned by your compulsion to be famous"), then expands to pinpoint the similar essence of human cruelty that enables soldiers to kill. As the narrator of "Doomed by the Numbers" explains: "the fact is people will still go on brutally/killing each other./Who will take my place and write about it?"

Ash concludes with an engaging, Rabelaisian roundelay of voices—mini-plays, summed up in just two stanzas, about complicated relationships between two people.

Once again, with *Ash*, Mindock proves herself to be unafraid of the dark. She is truly a leading, contemporary master of the edgy.

—**Karen Friedland**, author of *Places That Are Gone*
and *Tales from the Teacup Palace*.

Passionate and observant, Gloria Mindock is a tragic poet. Her books are wounds revisited. She knows that nothing, never heals.

"With a rolling pin in my hand, I roll your heart out flat… stop it from beating. The redness of blood turns to wax, sticky while wet." (Baked)

She senses the pain of the world in her being.

"The void looms deep, scorched like the desert blowing aimlessly." (Exit)

As her latest book *Ash* attests without doubt, Gloria is both a warrior and a martyr. Her words are swords that slowly transform into tears.

Her anger at life's injustice is mighty, but mighty is her generosity and her openness towards repair, harmony and universal peace. A must-read *Ash* conducts the reader through thorny labyrinths of pain and despair, allowing now and then a glimpse of ultimate resolve and liberation in verses of a rare beauty:

"…but gravity is about to free me into space… People will look at me day and night and ask, "what is it?" There is no control over what happens. The cathedral is high and my freckles fell on the floor as I left. Paleness now, that no one sees, but in the universe, I will be a prism." (Gravity)

"…A hunger surrounds us, dust gathers, and is wiped off, space evading all this as songs of the wind come through the window and we all hum." (Room)

—**Flavia Cosma**, author of *In the Arms of the Father*,
Val-David, QC

Glass Lyre Press

exceptional works to replenish the spirit

Glass Lyre Press is an independent literary publisher interested in technically accomplished, stylistically distinct, and original work. Glass Lyre seeks diverse writers that possess a dynamic aesthetic and an ability to emotionally and intellectually engage a wide audience of readers.

Glass Lyre's vision is to connect the world through language and art. We hope to expand the scope of poetry and short fiction for the general reader through exceptionally well-written books, which evoke emotion, provide insight, and resonate with the human spirit.

Poetry Collections
Poetry Chapbooks
Select Short & Flash Fiction
Anthologies

www.GlassLyrePress.com

CPSIA information can be obtained
at www.ICGtesting.com
Printed in the USA
BVHW070413080821
613574BV00002B/9

9 781941 783757